First and last; the tank the arsenal first made, the M-3 General Grant and (below) the 45-ton Pershing with 90 mm gun.

"TANKS
are Mighty Fine Things"

*How Chrysler's Detroit Tank Arsenal Built
the Tanks That Helped Win WWII*

by
Wesley W. Stout

for the
Chrysler Corporation
Detroit, Michigan 1946

Foreword

THE *tanks discussed in this book and the other weapons with which this war was won were the products of the intelligent cooperation of those who designed them, those who used them and those who made them. Ordnance approached industry as a recognized*

*partner in the development as well as the
making of new weapons and found industry
eager to pool its experience and ingenuity
with the Army's own skills.*

K. T. KELLER
President

*The Chrysler tank arsenal as seen from the
parking lot. It now is a permanent Army arsenal.*

The tank which whipped Rommel, the M-3. Note the two cannon, the larger in a sponson on the lower right hand side. (Below) How Plant Engineering plans a factory. Every machine tool of the arsenal layout was spotted in this factory.

From the Pacific in 1944, Pfc. Frank Upton of the Marine Corps sent this message to his old sergeant, William Hendricks, then on recruiting duty in Detroit:

"If you should go to the Chrysler tank arsenal, I want you to find the head man and kiss him on the forehead for me."

Private Upton went on to explain: "I love tanks and everybody connected with them. When I was hit on Tinian we were on patrol and the Nips had pinned us down in a field of sugar cane. They were in caves in the cliffs and while we could see exactly nothing of them, they were really giving us the business. A machine gun slug went through my hip early and I had visions of being in the field until dark, when one of those Chrysler jobs rolled up. The driver told me what he was going to do and after I had crawled out on harder ground, he drove the tank over me and pulled me through the escape hatch in the belly of the tank. Those treads looked plenty big as they straddled me, but we drove back to the lines slick as a whistle.

"Tanks are mighty fine things—mighty fine!"

* * *

First and biggest of America's defense plants was the Chrysler tank arsenal in 1941. Bigger were built later, but the arsenal continued to be the nation's most spectacular war plant, its best production show, the first every distinguished visitor asked to see. History was made there.

From it came 25,059 medium and heavy tanks of twelve different types, including the tanks which first turned the tide of the war, in North Africa for the British.

Of these, 22,234 were new, 2,825 were rebuilt. This was twice the number of all B-17 Flying Fortresses built for the Air Force.

The size of the tanks built there grew from 23 tons to 65 tons.

The Chrysler tank contract approached the two billion dollar mark at its peak. The estimated total after cutbacks due to the defeat of the Axis was $1,350,000,000. This figure included 3,126 car lots of

2

Chrysler's first tank snaps a telephone pole at 1941's Presentation Day ceremony. Note employees on the roof.

service replacement parts shipped from the arsenal, the equivalent of a freight train more than 31 miles long.

The Corporation returned to the Government in voluntary cash refunds and price reductions more than $50,000,000. How much more it is not possible to say because costs fluctuated constantly due to volume and to engineering changes.

For planning and directing the building and equipment of the arsenal, Chrysler was paid a fee of $4.

The Chrysler Engineering Ordnance Division, under the direction of O. R. Skelton, carried out more than 1,150 engineering projects for Army Ordnance, including the design and building of 38 pilot tanks of new types, and the operation of an Ordnance proving grounds.

The original arsenal was expanded more than half again in 1942 to 1,248,321 square feet, yet the contract overflowed into twelve other Chrysler plants and at its peak came to employ close to 25,000 Chrysler workers and 3,200,000 feet of Chrysler space, this exclusive of thousands of sub-contractors scattered over the nation.

Many war-built plants ended as surplus to the Government. Due to advance planning by Ordnance and Chrysler, the Corporation was able to turn over to the Army in 1945, a modern, self-contained factory for the peacetime design, repair, building and testing of armored vehicles, a permanent addition to the Army's arsenals.

Maj. General C. M. Wesson, then Chief of Ordnance, and Chrysler Corporation's President K. T. Keller at the microphone when tank No. 1 was delivered to the Army.

In a critical shortage of tank engines, Chrysler Engineering put five standard automobile motors on a common shaft to power 7,600 tanks. In the unprecedented time of nine months from the first discussion, the Corporation was making tanks with this multibank engine.

Arsenal test track drivers, driving 24 hours a day in all weather throughout the war, logged a mileage of more than fifty times around the earth, this not including the Tank Arsenal Proving Grounds' test driving.

The Chrysler tank contract began with an order

5

dated August 15, 1940, for 1,000 M2A1 23-ton tanks to be delivered by August, 1942, at the rate of 100 a month. It specified that the arsenal was to be completed by September, 1941.

Thirteen days after the contract was placed, Ordnance scrapped the M2A1 design and substituted the 28-ton M3, as yet undesigned. Yet Chrysler made

Shipping and heavy repairs were crowded into one bay before the arsenal was expanded.

the first two M3 pilot tanks in April, 1941, made its first production tank in July, had delivered more than 500 before Pearl Harbor and all of the first 1,000 by January 26, 1942, eight months ahead of schedule.

But before it could build the first production M3's, the Army was asking Chrysler by June, 1941, to double its schedule for that first year. By September the Army was asking the Corporation to expand tank output to 750 monthly, seven and a half times the goal set in the original contract, and to change over to the 32-ton Sherman M4 model. By January of 1942, Chrysler was tooling to build 1,000 tanks monthly at the Army's urgent request. This production never was reached only because it no longer was needed after 1942.

Chrysler had delivered 3,100 M3 tanks on July 10, 1942, first anniversary of the first production tank. Twelve days later the arsenal made its first M4 and in another twelve days this Sherman type had entirely replaced the M3 on the assembly lines.

The changeover from the M3 to the M4 was accomplished in the midst of the expansion of the arsenal by 50% in size and the removal of 776 large machine tools from the arsenal to nine other Chrysler plants, without an interruption of production.

The Sherman was replaced in 1945 by the 43-ton Pershing tank and had the war continued into 1946 the arsenal would have been making still later types weighing up to 65 tons.

The arsenal rebuilt into first line fighters 2,825

tanks that had been used in the training of our armored divisions, replacing all worn parts and installing all late engineering changes, a job turned over in 1944 to the Evansville Chrysler plant for lack of space and labor in Detroit. The British got 1,610 of these and they formed the greater part of the British armored strength in Italy.

Chrysler sold $41,000,000 of tank parts to some 95 other contractors building tanks and tank components, largely in the first two years of operation.

"We have upped the ante on you time and again and you have met every demand," Lt. Gen. Levin H. Campbell, Jr., Chief of Ordnance, told the arsenal force in 1942 in presenting them with the first Army-Navy E flag awarded in Detroit, the first to any tank contractor.

"Surely, when the history of the war is written, this job will rank without a peer," General Campbell wrote Mr. Keller in April, 1943.

"Your plant is the most outstanding example of big, bold, imaginative planning I have ever seen," a British Purchasing Commission officer said.

"This is the most amazing production job I have ever seen," Donald Nelson said after touring the plant with President Roosevelt.

Lt. Col. Joseph M. Colby, as chief of the Development section of the Detroit Ordnance District, was the man through whom new tank design came. Speaking of the men who translated these drawings into tanks, he said, "All engaged to make something they

8

never had seen. They were frustrated and exasperated by late drawings and changes of design, shortages of everything they needed, late deliveries and engineering bugs, yet we never heard a bitter word from them. For such men I have, as a soldier and a citizen, the highest respect."

* * *

The Nazis were rolling relentlessly down upon Paris on June 7, 1940 when Lieutenant General Knudsen, recently drafted from General Motors to command the national defense program, phoned Mr.

General Grant (M-3) tanks and crews training for Africa in California's Mojave desert in 1942.

Keller from Washington. The General said he would be in Detroit over the week-end and wished urgently to see Chrysler's president.

They met Sunday morning on Grosse Ile. "How would Chrysler like to build some tanks for the Army?" asked Knudsen.

Keller said yes. This is a decision which he ordinarily would have referred to the directors. But three months earlier it had been apparent that America must rearm and he had then advised the directors that such a program demanded Chrysler's active participation. They had authorized management to take any job which it could do with satisfaction to

Horizontal volute suspension arms moving by conveyor belt down the arsenal machine line.

The arsenal was President Roosevelt's first stop on his 1942 secret tour of war plants and army camps. In the car with him are former Michigan Governor Murray D. Van Wagoner, Mrs. Roosevelt, Mr. Keller and War Production Chief Donald M. Nelson.

Assembling tank tracks. Tanks began with rubber shoes, were forced to shift to steel for lack of rubber.

the Government and with credit to the Corporation.

Keller asked where his men could see a tank and Knudsen proposed that Chrysler send a group to Washington Tuesday to talk with Army Ordnance. The next morning Keller put the Corporation to work looking for possible tank arsenal sites, and on Tuesday morning he and other Chrysler executives were in Washington conferring with General Wesson, then Chief of Ordnance.

Washington had no tank to show the Detroiters. They would have to go to the Rock Island, Illinois, arsenal to see one. Rock Island was building three pilot models of the new M2A1 tank of which the Army said it wanted 1,500 as quickly as it could get them. General Wesson estimated that it would take practically two years to complete such an order.

On Wednesday the Chrysler party was in Rock Island and first saw a tank, an M2A1 without armor. They had hoped to take back to Detroit a set of blueprints, weighing 186 pounds. They could get only a few, however, the balance reaching Detroit by express in a packing case on Monday, June 17th.

That night a specially chosen group of men, the nucleus of the tank arsenal organization, went to work in secrecy on the bare top floor of the Dodge Conant Avenue building. Their job was to produce an estimate, in four and a half weeks, of the cost of making this monster in quantities, land, buildings and machinery included. They worked seven days a week from 8:30 a.m. until 11 p.m. for five days, knocked off at 6 p.m. on Saturdays and at 5:30 on Sundays.

Such tanks as Rock Island had produced were made by tool room methods necessarily, and these were Rock Island blueprints, some in ⅛th scale. To insure that automobile men would grasp the size of every tank piece, to insure that

Sir John Dill, British Field Marshal, signing the arsenal visitors' book.

A Fifth Army tank unit poised in the Pietramalu area, Italy, and ready to strike.

production parts would assemble as designed, the Corporation ordered an exact reproduction or "mock-up" as the engineers call it of an M2A1 tank made in wood. The pattern shops were instructed to drill all holes and to shellac the finished model.

There was a dual purpose in the shellac; one for protection of the wood, and two if it should be scraped away at any point when the pieces were joined, this would advertise the fact that some part had not been accurately designed and had not fitted without adjustment. But this wooden model pieced together precisely; there was no scratch on any part. The United States still was a long way from war, but

Herringbone final drive reduction gears passing down a line of gear shapers.

the model was guarded zealously, and only a few knew what the men on the 8th. floor were up to.

Where were the tanks to be built? No available buildings existed in the Detroit area which would house the job. The Army had at that time been given only a third of the money it wanted for tanks and it wished naturally to put these dollars, not into buildings, but into tanks, of which it had built just eighteen, no two alike, between 1919 and 1938. There was no Defense Plant Corporation, no 5-year amortization as yet.

Mr. Keller's mind went back to the previous war in which Dodge Brothers had made recoil mechanisms for the 155-mm cannon in a building put up by the Government on Lynch Road. When the war ended, the Army had asked the Dodges to take the building off its hands.

John Dodge said that they did not want the building, but the Government pressed it on them at something like 30 cents on the dollar, crating the machinery and sending it to the Rock Island arsenal for storage. The Dodge Brothers estimated that the cost of crating and shipping was more than the Army had got for the property.

On that June, 1940, trip to Rock Island to see a tank, Fred Lamborn had noted there a large pile of the 155-mm recoil mechanisms which he had helped to make at Lynch Road in 1917-18. For 22 years these big gun parts had been stacked there like cord wood, laid down in heavy grease. Through all these years a detail of men had "exercised" the mechanisms methodically, starting at one end of the stack and working through it, then doing it again. The visit of the Chrysler party coincided with Dunkirk. England feared imminent invasion and was tragically short of weapons. A few days after Lamborn saw them, most of these recoils were rushed to Britain to bolster her coastal defenses.

This experience suggested an idea which Mr. Keller carried to Washington. "Why don't you have a tank arsenal?" he proposed to General Wesson. "With the increasing role of tanks in war, you are going to need a place where you can design, build, test and repair tanks. A good place for this piece of permanent apparatus would be in Detroit alongside such a pool of labor as we have at Chrysler. Have the arsenal set up and ready to run. When you want tanks, we move in and make tanks for you; when you no longer want tanks, we move back and, pray God, make automobiles."

"That's exactly what we want—a self-contained, permanent tank arsenal machining even its own armor plate," said General Wesson, "and maybe the Army can find the money for it."

On July 17, 1940, just a month from the receipt of the blueprints, the estimate was complete. It was based upon an output of ten tanks a day. When the Army reviewed the cost, it counted the money in its purse and cut the capacity to five daily. Also for economy's sake, it threw out the armor plate machining equipment as a detail which could be left to the mills.

The estimate now had to be refigured. This was done and shortly Chrysler had a letter of intent to make 1,000 tanks by August, 1942. The Government would pay for the land and plant, leasing it to Chrysler which would superintend construction and equipment. The price of the tank would be $33,500, a fixed price bid in which the Corporation was protected by an escalator clause against rising labor and materials costs. The plant was to be ready by September 15, 1941, production to rise from three tanks in the twelfth month to 100 in the 15th. month and thereafter through 23 months.

Ordnance and Chrysler had agreed upon a site of 113 acres some 17 miles from downtown Detroit, a farm occupied by renters. The farmhouse and barn

Receiving dock crowded with parts for the new Pershing tank early in 1945.

stood where the administration building was to rise. The land was in corn, buckwheat and onions. There was no public transportation, but in 1940 any Detroiter who owned a pair of shoes owned a car. Warren township had been purely agricultural, its boast that it was the Winter rhubarb capital of Michigan. It still is a rural countryside. The tank arsenal offices looked out upon a wheat field throughout the war, and the roar of tanks never drowned the barnyard sounds.

Abruptly on August 28, 1940, the General Staff concluded that the M2A1 was not good enough and an improved and larger tank to be known as the M3 should be designed at once. Reports from Europe indicated that the M2A1 would be obsolete before it was built. Too, the War Department had made up its mind to reorganize our mechanized cavalry and infantry into an armored force on the Panzer pattern. A new and then large appropriation by the Congress had made this possible.

This need not hold up Chrysler, Ordnance said; the contract would be altered later. But the arsenal staff were stopped in their tracks, for they now were about to build something which

Mrs. Henry Morgenthau presenting the arsenal with a Minute Man flag for bond sales.

Brig. Gen. G. F. Doriot, Chrysler's Vice President and Vice Chairman of the Board Fred M. Zeder, Lt. Col. J. M. Colby, Detroit Ordnance Research Chief and Chrysler's Director of Engineering O. R. Skelton.

had not yet begun to take shape in outline on the drawing board. Complete prints would not be ready before Thanksgiving at the earliest. Until they had their prints, the staff could not know, of course, what kind and how many tools they needed.

The buildings could be put up, anyway, and ground was broken September 9, 1940. How big should it be? Here had been a question for a fortune teller. Would we be dragged into the war or not? Tanks never had been built on a production basis. There were no past performance charts to go by. If the plant should turn out to be too small, that would be awkward; if too large, Chrysler would look foolish.

Ed Hunt was given the job of getting the arsenal tooled. Tooling it well, he then was given the job of running it. As his chief engineer, Elmer Dodt was sent at once to the Aberdeen Proving Grounds where

21

the M3 was being designed. It was his job to snatch the layout drawings from the boards and shoot vandykes or copies to Detroit, or to phone any information he could pick up.

The Army welcomed Dodt's suggestions and literally hundreds of drawings were revised in their first state to provide for cheaper, faster, easier manufacture on a production line. There being no place to live in Aberdeen, Dodt stayed at a hotel in Havre de Grace. Once a week he would fly back to Detroit to report. On the six other days he would airmail his vandykes or phone his data to Detroit, and the

Three British veterans of El Alamein, Generals Briggs, Davidson and Galehouse, and Brigadier Ross, commanding the British war office in Detroit.

arsenal was tooled on such fragmentary information.

Late at night a tourist putting in at the Havre de Grace inn might be startled to find the lobby floor covered with prints, and a man, phone in hand, walking among them and barking dimensions and other technical jabberwocky into the mouthpiece. It would be Dodt talking to Conant Avenue. The Ordnance design engineers worked nightly, often past midnight, and their hours were Dodt's.

The Autumn was wet, the early Winter abnormally cold, but the buildings rose to schedule, the foundations emerging from a morass of mud and shivering cornstalks. As late as December 20th., the design of the M3 was only 90% complete and final prints and parts lists were not promised before January 30, 1941. There were worse worries. The reader who supposes that there were no delays, shortages and bottlenecks before Pearl Harbor has forgotten that American industry already was manufacturing at a great rate for the British and Russians under private agreement, and that the tank program was one detail only of a vast American rearmament authorized that summer by the Congress.

Machine tools were tighter in 1940 than they were in the midst of the war, both because of demand and the fact that the machine tool industry had not yet expanded to its swollen later size. So the equipment of the arsenal was a long and ceaseless battle. Before mid-October, about 60% of this equipment was on order despite incomplete engineering information.

Ordering it was easy, getting it was hard.

Late in January the steel of the main building was up. The roof and sidewalls of one-third of it were hurried into place and the first little group of foremen and superintendents moved in. As the power house was unfinished, a passenger locomotive was rented and run into this section. Its steam, plus salamanders and canvas curtains, made the space barely habitable. The men worked in overcoats and wore gloves much of the time.

As the days grew longer, Mr. Keller began to press for an estimated date for the pilot tank. The arsenal named Easter Sunday. Late in March, the monster began to take shape, the floor plates the first to be joined. There were no cranes as yet, so two plant jitneys lifted the great plates onto steel "horses." The armor plates being unchecked, it was necessary to bolt the tank together to see if the plates fitted. To his delight, Keller one day saw what looked like a completed job, only to find his baby scattered over the shop floor when he returned the next day.

But on Good Friday, April 11, 1941, the pilot tank was driven gingerly 20 feet forward and backward in the shop. Growing bolder, the staff maneuvered it outside on the concrete apron. The shop looked like no-man's land, the floor pitted with foundation holes for machines, and there was one door only which could be used, but chalk lines were laid out for the driver to follow.

The next day, a day ahead of the promise, the pilot

Tank transmission case machine line. Only heavy machining remained at the arsenal after expansion plans put many operations in other Chrysler plants.

tank was brought outside officially with the late Ray Clark at the helm and K. T. Keller alongside him. Clark had come from Rock Island where he had driven light tanks.

After the test run and the departure of Mr. Keller and his party, the boys took their tank out for another spin. The watchman's temporary shack still stood at the front gate, a sort of sentry box. In the door and filling it stood a big Plant Protection guard munching a sandwich and looking on interestedly.

Either unprepared for the dash and power of the M3 or intending to scare the watchman and misjudging his distance, Clark brushed the sentry box with the tank, overturning the box and guard.

The unfinished Chrysler arsenal had only 230 hourly workers on the payroll that April 12th.

The first pilot was presented to the Government by Chrysler dealers as a gift at a show attended by Generals Wesson, Campbell, Barnes, Knudsen and Chaffee, the Mayor and Governor Van Wagoner. The 2,000 guests and employees watched No. 1 snap telephone poles in three pieces, smash through a small woods, plunge through a pond and pierce a 2-story frame building so much like a bullet that this stunt was unsatisfying. But on a return trip, the tank made matchwood of the house.

Unknown to the Ordnance chiefs present, the arsenal had completed a second pilot tank. As No. 1 was taking its bows, No. 2 came out shooting, its 75-mm and 37-mm rifles barking, its machine guns chattering, to join its twin, and the crowd broke into spontaneous yells. It was smart showmanship. The second tank, like the first, was complete to the last detail.

The first tank was shipped to Aberdeen May 3rd. At Mr. Keller's suggestion, the second was held at the arsenal. There would be many late engineering changes and Chrysler wished to incorporate these in

Chrysler-built Sherman tank slugging its way through Northern France.

a pilot tank before production should begin. Pilot No. 1 remained at Aberdeen throughout the war, but it led a rugged life there. By January of 1943 when it had logged 7,000 miles in the testing of M3 components, it was made a target for new armor-piercing anti-tank guns and projectiles. One of its major wounds still is visible on its lower left flank. Next it was turned over to the Ordnance school for the training of tank-recovery companies. These lads gaily rolled it over cliffs and into ditches in order to pull it out and patch it up again.

It had been tagged for the scrap heap when Elmer Dodt spied it one day in the Spring of 1945 and got General Harris' approval for its return to Chrysler as a permanent exhibit. It rolled into the arsenal again

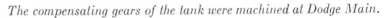

The compensating gears of the tank were machined at Dodge Main.

in June, 1945, honorably discharged. When the tank contract was terminated, it was sent to Highland Park where, during reconversion, it stood in the yard almost hidden among stacks of axle housings.

By early June of 1941 the Government was urging that the arsenal be put to work 24 hours a day quickly, by January 1, 1942, at the latest. To understand Washington's pressure, remember that the Selective Service Act now had been passed. The

Another machine operation performed at Dodge, the suspension wheels.

Army's equipment needs had leaped and it had more money to spend than it had dreamed of a year earlier.

A month later Chrysler was given a letter contract for 1,600 additional tanks and sixteen sets of spare parts, the latter a big order in itself. So before the

Sherman M-4 tank posed for action. Chrysler built nearly 18,000 Sherman type tanks alone.

One of De Soto's jobs was machining the piston rods of the gun recoils.

arsenal could get into production, it was outgrowing its clothing. The first production tank came off the assembly line July 8th. Six more were shipped that month as scheduled.

The Army now wanted another 1,200 M3 tanks before January. Though the M3 was just entering production, everyone knew that a new medium tank, the M4, had been designed and would replace the M3. A Chrysler group headed by Vice President B. E. Hutchinson carried the Corporation's revised M3 schedule to Washington, however, August 15, 1941. This called for 7 tanks in July, 50 in August, 100 in October, 125 in November and 150 by December. Mr. Hutchinson also presented a 7-day, 24-hour schedule, but recommended a 6-day week as allowing a safety margin, to which General Lewis agreed.

The next day the arsenal went to a 6-day around-the-clock schedule and three assembly lines were working. Figuring on an orderly operation to build 1,000 tanks under pre-war conditions by August of 1942, the arsenal had planned to add a second shift around Thanksgiving, a third in February. But under the new schedule new labor began to flood in on the plant at the rate of 100 a day, or as fast as Personnel could clear them. The working force which had been 2,107 on July 24th., passed 4,000 on August 9th. and 5,000 on the 25th.

This was not a construction job where a new man could be handed a shovel and told to dig. Each had to be trained. The only solution was to assign two men to every existing machine, an old one to teach, a new one to learn.

General Campbell told Mr. Keller on September 8th. that the using arms were enthusiastic about the M4 (Sherman) design and wanted it put into production just as quickly as might be done without slowing M3 output. Chrysler was asked to build two pilot Sherman tanks. A week later, Generals Christmas and Lewis were asking Mr. Keller to submit a proposal to manufacture M4 tanks, reaching 750 monthly at the earliest possible moment.

In order to build 750 tanks monthly, Chrysler would have to move all but final assembly and the heavier machining into twelve other Corporation plants, and to find many new sub-contractors.

Though the arsenal would be extended 450-feet in length, with another 100-foot bay added along the whole 1,850-foot length, less than a quarter of the tank job, by cost, would remain there, exclusive of armor plate and motors, which had been purchased all along. Thenceforth the arsenal was one of thirteen Chrysler tank plants, so to speak. Though no one then foresaw that all automobile production would cease in four months, production already had been cut pro rata and there would be room in Chrysler factories.

As a tank engine, Ordnance was using an adapted Curtiss-Wright radial air-cooled aircraft motor. In June when Knudsen had paid a visit to Chrysler Engineering, he had warned Keller that aircraft engine manufacturing capacity was very tight and would be increasingly so, what with the ballooning Army and Navy air forces programs. Training planes would eat up as many motors as service planes. Moreover, the M4 would be five tons heavier than the M3 and the 9-cylinder Wright was not quite powerful enough for the added load.

Could Chrysler, he asked, work out a tank engine which could be made on machines and tools existing in its plants?

Two years is par for a new motor. The only possible quick solution would be to use an existing automobile engine in multiple, one with a long background of successful use and already tooled. In the Chrysler division, the Corporation had just such a motor and

34

a tool-up. Engineering combined five Chrysler
6-cylinder motors on a common crankshaft. The
design began with the premise of making a minimum
number of changes in a standard car engine, this for
greater speed of production. With such limitations,
it would not be an ideal tank engine, the Corporation
warned the Army, yet it turned out to be a fine motor
for the Sherman tank.

Affectionately known to the armored forces as
"The Egg Beater" or as "The Dionne Quints," this
multibank engine drove 7,500 Sherman tanks. Five

*Ambassador Averill Harriman, Donald Nelson and British
Minister of Supply, Oliver Lyttleton, with Mr. Keller.*

thousand additional motors were built as spares. In a competitive test at Aberdeen which began October 11, 1943, and continued until February 10, 1944, four M4A4 tanks with Chrysler multibank engines were entered against four tanks of each of three other engine types. Three of the four Chrysler-powered tanks completed the 4,000 mile marathon. Of the other twelve, only one finished. Ordnance reported that the Chrysler motor gave the most reliable performance, that its maintenance requirement was lowest, its power loss after 400 miles negligible. Its oil consumption was bettered only by a Diesel tank engine.

The first experimental multibank motor was installed in a tank November 15, 1941, and ran all Winter in a test of 4,000 miles. It was well that the engineers had moved swiftly, for by September 19th., H. L. Weckler was phoning Brigadier General Jack K. Christmas, deputy commander and Chief of Industrial operations of the Detroit office of the Chief of Ordnance, that the motor shortage was disturbing. In nineteen days the arsenal had received only four Wright engines. Though the motor shortage never actually halted the assembly lines, it was touch and go until the multibank motor was in production the next Spring.

These were the days when the national spotlight seldom lifted from the arsenal. As the first and still

Infantry cautiously moving into action behind the cover of a Sherman tank.

the only big defense plant, it was the apple of Uncle Sam's eye. Everyone promoted it like a 4-ring circus. A year earlier it had been a cornfield and now it was the Arsenal of Democracy. Train loads of writers,

Maj. Gen. A. C. Gillem signing the arsenal register, Major General Levin H. Campbell, Jr., Chief of Ordnance, succeeding General Wesson, with glasses.

editors and radio commentators on conducted tours came, saw and exclaimed.

Seeking the superlative, they liked to dwell upon the 750 tanks monthly the plant would be making in 1942. Chrysler sometimes was made uneasy by such publicity. The Corporation would have preferred it to have followed rather than preceded the performance.

38

But when reporters were asked: "Why don't you wait until we have done it? That's the time to talk about it", they would reply: "But it wouldn't be news then."

Tank No. 500 was shipped from the arsenal December first. The country still was at peace. Then came Pearl Harbor. Now Washington began to talk about 1,000 tanks monthly from Chrysler. Two days after New Years, Mr. Weckler was in the capital to attend an OPM meeting to stress the necessity of all-out tank production. It was feared then that thousands of tanks might be needed to repel invasion. The chairman of the meeting gave Chrysler a new schedule calling for 275 tanks in January, rising to 480 in April and 800 by September, or almost as many monthly as the arsenal originally had been asked to make in two years.

As Vice President responsible for all manufacturing, Weckler could not accept so irrational a schedule. The designed capacity of the plant was 13½ tanks a day, working 24 hours, and all tools for this output were not yet in. Machinery was on order to bring this capacity to 750 monthly plus spare parts, but under OPM allocations the Corporation would not get this added machinery in time to reach 750 before December. Of course, if OPM could give him all the tools he wanted by September, Chrysler could be making 1,000 tanks a month by January, 1943, but this was idle dreaming.

The chairman said that he realized that the schedule was not practicable, but that it was vital to set a high objective to shoot at. Chrysler was asked to figure its barest machine requirements for 1,000 tanks monthly, also to see what it could do toward finding equipment to make 250 additional final-drives, volute suspensions, rear idlers and sprockets each, or, better still, 500 more of each for other tank contractors. General Christmas asked Weckler to shift from the M3 to the Sherman M4 tank at M3 No. 3,352.

In early January Mr. Weckler carried to Washington an estimate of some $26,000,000 for the added facilities with which to reach 1,000 tanks monthly, plus extra components for other tank builders; and $3,500,000 for the additional tools needed to produce 1,000 Chrysler 5-bank motors a month. General Campbell said that he was under constant pressure to expand no more plants in areas as susceptible to air attack as Detroit was believed to be. Weckler demonstrated that this expansion really would decentralize the tank contract to Chrysler plants as far removed as Kokomo and Newcastle, Indiana, and to many other points outside the Detroit region.

OPM phoned its approval of both estimates on February 18, 1942, and now the struggle for tools began all over.

Tank No. 1,100 was one of a load shipped February 9th. to Boston for Russia where it helped to stem the Nazi onslaught that summer.

When the arsenal had produced 300 tanks in March by the 25th., 75 better than any previous month, General Campbell wired: "This is especially gratifying to me as it is always nice to back a winner." In the remaining six days of March, 66 more tanks were built. By April 22nd., one year after the presentation of the first pilot M3 to the Army, Chrysler had built more than 2,000 tanks, twice the goal set by the Government originally for the following August.

July 10th. was the first anniversary of the first

Machining the 75 mm gun mounts at the arsenal.

production M3 tank. On that day Tank No. 3,100 was christened. The first production M4 was completed July 22nd., and on August 3rd. the last M3 rang down the curtain on the first act of the tank drama. News photographers snapped the last of the Old Guard alongside the first of the bigger, tougher

*Maj. Gen. A. W. Richardson of the Lucas Mission
(British) lowering himself into a tank hatch.*

M4's, which had been held at the arsenal for the
occasion.

Oddly, the M3's firepower was greater than that of
its bigger, heavier-armored successor. It was the most
heavily armed vehicle for its weight ever known to
war. But it had the drawback of carrying its knock-
out weapon, the 75-mm rifle, well down on the right
hand side where its angle of fire was restricted. The
place for the gun was in the turret from where it
could fire in any direction. As there was no room
there for it and the 37-mm cannon too, the 37-mm

was sacrificed in the M4.

The changeover was made without "losing a tank." The Detroit Times commented: "One of the most remarkable achievements of the automobile manufacturers has been in the tank field. It was a product of which they knew nothing. Chrysler took over this job. It is seven months ahead of schedule on its first order and its present capacity was not even considered possible when it was given its first contract. Since then it has changed over to the new all-welded hull (this was only one of many changes) without interrupting output. If ever the ingenuity of the industry met its test it has been on this job."

Chrysler-Jefferson put five automobile engines on a common crankshaft to power 7,600 tanks.

The ultimate accolade came August 10. 1942, when General Campbell awarded the arsenal the first of the E flags. The general spoke from a flat car beneath the guns of a battery of Shermans to the assembled employees. "We have upped the ante on you time and again and you have met every demand," said he.

How was it done? Between February 7th. and September 5th. 776 large machine tools were transferred to nine other Chrysler plants. Moving 776 machine tools over a period of a few months is just another job if nothing else is involved. The trick was so to move them as never to interfere with either the old M3 or

Welding the front hull section of the Pershing tank at the Plymouth plant.

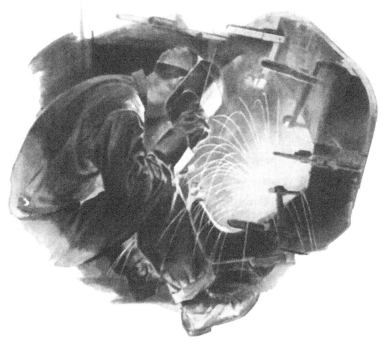

Close-up of an electric-arc welder at work.

the new M4 production. This took a timetable as
adroit as that for moving an army over a single-track
railroad. Except for the heaviest machines and those
shifted out of Detroit, no tool missed a day's work.

None could be moved until an adequate bank of
parts had been built up at the arsenal to protect the
assembly lines. One part might involve 60 machines.
In such a case, machines representing, say, the first
ten operations would be worked overtime to produce
a surplus of partly machined pieces, then trucked to
another plant while the machines for the remaining
operations were held at the arsenal until the stock

45

board listed a safe reserve of finished parts. The volute suspension job was two months in making its way some eight miles to Lynch Road.

The first whittling down of the 1,000-a-month program came in September, 1942, when tank schedules for 1942 were cut 40% across the board for lack of steel, needed for ships. Then, on November 18th. Gen. A. G. Quinton wired the Corporation to suspend all further expansion of the arsenal due to "changes in military requirements." Chrysler then lacked 177 machines of its needs for 800-a-month, plus spares and extra final-drives and transmissions. Ordnance allowed the arsenal 31 of these machines with which to balance out the lines.

Despite this curtailment, the arsenal in December broke all production records and at Ordnance's urging, turning out 896 tanks, more than its total for 1941, almost double any previous month and an all-time record. Ordnance had seen in November that it was not going to get 15,000 tanks in 1942, the goal it had set after the 40% cut. As Chrysler alone had met its schedule, this over-all deficit could be overcome in the six weeks remaining only by the arsenal, which was beseeched to make 1,380 tanks in November and December. The 15,000 goal was met with four to spare.

The tank plant was awarded a white star in February, 1943, for its Army-Navy E flag for "con-

Tanks ranged in line for massed artillery fire, seldom done by our Army, often by the Germans.

tinuous meritorious services on the production front," the first large war plant so honored. "You have continued to maintain the high standard you have set for yourselves," said Under Secretary of War Patterson. "You may well be proud of your achievement."

And in April General Campbell wrote Mr. Keller: "Words, of course, are totally inadequate to describe how we in Ordnance feel about the accomplishments of the Chrysler tank arsenal."

Despite this praise, tank orders were falling in the Spring of 1943; production had overtaken the Army's needs. Dwindling schedules were tempered, however, by the return from various depots for modification

General Jacob L. Devers, who was Commanding General U. S. Seventh Army in France, with Mr. Zeder and Mr. Keller.

of 809 Sherman tanks. These were going to the British, who wanted many changes made. The rebuilds enabled the arsenal to set a new one day record on May 12th. with 87 tanks shipped, but 56 of these were modifications. The last of this group were reshipped June 14, 1943, and shortly the first 1,423 Shermans on which many of our armored forces had been trained began to return home for a complete reconditioning job before being sent into battle.

In May, 1942, the Corporation voluntarily had cut the tank price $1,000 each, though it was making tanks on a fixed price contract. A year later Chrysler dropped a check for $7,876,000 unannounced into the Government's lap, a rebate made possible by December's record output. Paradoxically, the Corporation sometimes increased the tank price on new orders while cutting it on past business. This was due less to constantly changing design than to changing quantities. The more a plant makes, the cheaper the unit cost should be whether the product is automobiles, lawn mowers or tanks.

New Sherman orders and a number of new tank types soon reversed the Spring's declining schedules. The new types included an order for 250 T23 electric-drive tanks, the direct progenitor of the Pershing. Ordnance and General Electric had been collaborating on the electric-drive for two years. It gave a high mobility, a speed of 35 miles an hour forward or in reverse, and the ability to pivot on a nickel. It also would have a bigger, harder-hitting gun. Ordnance regarded its two tons of additional weight over the Sherman as its only disadvantage.

The using arms did not agree. They held that the T23's electric propulsion demanded crews of skilled electricians and so no T23 ever left this country and no second order was placed. An order for Shermans with a radial Diesel engine had a similar fate. The using arms wished to limit the supply problem to one grade of fuel, 80-octane gasoline. Only 75 of these were built.

Another new type mounted a 105-mm howitzer, then the heaviest gun ever carried by any medium

Pre-battle check of equipment by a British tank unit in Italy. The tank was Chrysler-built.

Forge shop of the Chrysler Newcastle, Indiana plant, which made many tank parts.

tank. It first was tested in September of 1942 and ordered into production in March, 1943. Weighing little more than the 75-mm gun, it threw a wicked, high-explosive shell at a high angle and was deadly for many uses where a cannon was impotent.

The difference between a howitzer and a gun is that between your rifle and your shotgun. To knock out another tank, the Army needed a gun with its armor-penetrating shell, but such a shell is like a rifle bullet —its miss is as good as a mile. There is no use in throwing it at infantry or at a battery of artillery. The howitzer with its demolition and fragmentation shell is powerless against tanks, but murderous to infantry and artillery and to such targets as buildings, through which a gun shell will simply rip a hole.

A fourth new type was a Sherman with a 76-mm gun and "wet stowage." The greatest single hazard in tank warfare is the explosion of a tank's own shells from enemy fire. Ordnance therefore decided to lay these shells down in ethylene glycol, the stuff you put in your car radiator in Winter. But the design necessary to liquid stowage reduced the amount of ammunition a tank could carry and, in the long run, the armored forces concluded that fewer shells was the greater evil.

Machining tank road wheel shafts at the Newcastle, Indiana, plant.

Wet stowage was abandoned, but the 76-mm gun was a much longer advance over the 75-mm than the one millimeter of caliber suggests. It had a much higher muzzle velocity, greater armor penetration and a fabulous accuracy.

Ordnance began to talk in the Summer of 1943 about introducing a high muzzle velocity 90-mm cannon on the electric-drive T23. As this long-barrelled gun would further increase the tank's weight, the Development section ordered the introduction of a new horizontal volute suspension and a wide (23-inch) track for a better ride and better flotation in mud.

The reader may remember that Ordnance was denounced by some critics in the latter stages of the war for the narrow (16½-inch) tracks of our tanks and our lack of high calibered, high velocity tank guns. Note that Ordnance had introduced both more than a year before. Chrysler Engineering had been given a project October 1, 1941, before Pearl Harbor, to develop this horizontal suspension which became standard on all medium tanks by August, 1944.

Again in 1943 the arsenal ended the year in a sprint. It was meeting its schedules, but in late November Ordnance again found that the Army was likely to miss its over-all tank quota, and appealed to Chrysler for an extra push in December. The Corporation promised to build 55 tanks beyond its schedule. Though schedules had fallen sharply after the first quarter, 1943 was the plant's peak year. It built 5,111 Shermans with the multibank motor,

1,528 with the aircraft motor, 16 Diesel-powered tanks and rebuilt 1,306 tanks for a total of 7,708 shipped in one year.

Except for 148 M4's, all of the plant's 1944 production was new in type, with all the unforeseen manufacturing difficulties always present in varying degrees on new models. This was the lesser part of it, however. When Chrysler had taken over the M4A3 tank the previous September from Ford, which was dropping out of tanks, it was on the understanding that it was to build this model as Ford had built it. But on reports from the field, Ordnance began to introduce a series of drastic changes, including dropping the 75-mm gun for the 76-mm and the 105-mm howitzer, wet stowage and a new front end.

Wet stowage alone affected 2,500 items, many of long-time procurement, and eventually enforced a complete tear-up of the turret interior. To change the gun is to change the turret. The new 2-piece rolled and cast armor combination front was a major change, and all foundries were chronically overloaded.

The Pershing tank appeared in the Spring of 1944 when Ordnance asked the Corporation to estimate its requirements for building 200 of these monthly as soon as possible, with the expectation that they would supersede the Sherman types in 1945 production.

The Pershing was a revolutionary design, a tank greater in armor and firepower than anything within 20 tons of its weight. It was to carry either a 90-mm

54

Maj. Gen. Sir L. H. Williams, British Chief Ordnance Services and Stores, with Mr. Keller and Staff Executive L. D. Cosart.

gun or the 105-mm howitzer, the former throwing an armor-piercing shell with a core of cemented carbide, the ultra hard material used almost universally nowadays for the machining of tough metals.

A new type of springing, twelve heavy steel torsion bars running the width of the tank and protected by its armor, replaced the horizontal volute suspension. The independently sprung wheels were demountable like an automobile wheel, where the wheels of the Sherman types could be changed only after the suspension brackets had been removed.

Though it was intended that the Pershing should replace the Sherman in production in 1945, Ordnance in mid-May of 1944 asked for increased schedules on

55

Hundreds of thousands of track end connectors were made at Newcastle.

all Sherman types for the balance of the year, this in anticipation of the invasion of France, coming on June 6th. Test mileage was lowered temporarily to 30 miles and Chrysler was permitted to bring in advance procurements of materials for 1945 if need be.

Four days after D Day there was an Ordnance-Industry meeting in Detroit. Colonel Cummings, just back from a Washington meeting of the combined chiefs of staff to decide on the 1945 tank program, reported that tank types had been reduced from 13 to 8, would be cut further to 6. By now all of the Services had been converted to the need of heavier armor and guns and wider tracks and had dropped their insistence on a 35-ton maximum weight. They would prefer all Pershing tanks if they could get them, he said.

They were asking for more Pershing 105-mm tanks than had been scheduled. Ordnance had intended that Grand Blanc should build the 105-mm version, Chrysler the 90-mm, but in view of the demand for the latter, Chrysler would be asked to build both types.

By June 6th. Ordnance was asking the Corporation what facilities it would need to double Pershing out-

Maj. Gen. Urico Gaspar Dutra (center), now President of Brazil, then Minister of War, watches the machining of a turret. With him are his two aides and R. T. Keller, Works Manager of the Arsenal at left and C. B. Thomas, President of the Company's Export Division, in the rear.

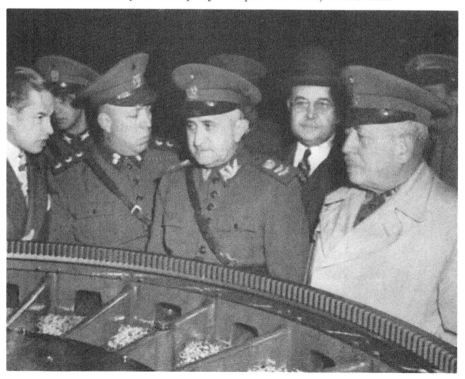

put to 400 a month, this in addition to increased Sherman schedules. At the same time, it wished another 1,000 tanks rebuilt. In view of the overload on the arsenal, it was decided to convert the Chrysler plant at Evansville, Indiana, just released from cartridge manufacture, to the rebuilding job.

When von Rundstedt found a hole in our line in December and came boring through, the Army appealed to Chrysler to better its December quota and to raise its sights on the Pershing tank from 400 to 500 monthly. The arsenal shipped 834 tanks that month, a mark exceeded only by December of 1942 when production was limited to one model.

This was a triumph over two new shortages—105-mm guns and flat cars. On Christmas day 75 tanks were ready to ship with only 18 flat cars on hand. The basic trouble was that the arsenal was competing with the Army itself for cars. Troop movements were eating up more and more of the railroads' overworked rolling stock. Ordnance ruled out 36, 37 and 38-foot flat cars for medium tanks. For Sherman types, 40 and 42-foot cars were specified. Two M3 tanks had been loaded on a 42-foot car, but every Sherman claimed a car to itself except when an infrequent 50-foot car turned up.

The Pershing, just around the corner now, would take a car with a minimum load limit of 118,000 pounds, eliminating many more. As for the T29 tank and the T92 and T93 mobile guns, coming up in 1946, they would weigh up to 68 tons with dunnage,

*A Chrysler-built Sherman tank helps to stim-
ulate war bond sales at Detroit's Air Show.*

demanding a car 9-feet, 2-inches wide with a minimum capacity of 160,000 pounds. These dimensions
would necessitate that the cars be moved only by
certain designated rail routes.

By the summer of 1945 when the Army was being
deployed from Europe to the Pacific and new tanks
were moving westward with them, the congestion
would have been truly serious if tank production had
not fallen greatly by then. Flat cars which had made

Maj. Gen. Marie Bethouart, French, at the arsenal with Major Robert J. Bedell, then commanding the arsenal. C. B. Thomas at far left and Matt Leonard, Tank Arsenal General Superintendent.

the round trip from Detroit to an Atlantic port in eight days normally were 26 to 30 days in reaching the West Coast and returning.

The drive to tool up for new and bigger tanks while straining to better Sherman schedules brought the total of Chrysler workers employed on tank work to 25,000 in December, 1944. Arsenal employment rose to 5,481, highest since the summer of 1942 before the contract had been scattered out. Another index of the pressure on the arsenal was its December electric and telephone bills. The electricity bill at the arsenal alone in December, 1942, when a record 813 tanks had been built, was $27,000. It was $32,351 in December, 1944. The phone bill which had been $6,095 two years earlier now was $9,071.

In September the Corporation had notified the Government that it would reduce the price of various tanks to be made after June 30, 1944, by a total of $10,926,879, due to economies and efficiencies.

Ordnance moved the Pershing goal up another notch in January, 1945, to 850 monthly. In the midst of this push for production on the new and much bigger tank, the Army introduced a new gun mount shield, front end casting and turret, final-drive and gear reduction on the Pershing, all major changes. These were no engineer's whims, but a military necessity. Ballistic tests had demonstrated that a gun shield and heavier frontal armor would be essential to the driver's protection, and the ratio of the final-drive gears was insufficient to handle this added weight.

The tank contract crossed the billion and a half dollar mark February 7th. A week later the Army Supply Program set a new mark for Chrysler in 1945 of 8,832 tanks. This would have been 2,176 more than the total of the biggest previous year. Even though Germany quit in May and Japan in August, 4,251 new tanks came off these assembly lines in 1945.

The new T80 track now was in production but could not be used on the earlier Sherman and Grant tanks without formidable altering of the tanks. This was out of the question, yet all our tanks needed wider tracks. As an answer, Chrysler Engineering designed

There were five assembly lines running at the peak of arsenal production in June, 1944. All in the photograph are Shermans.

the grouser, a sort of steel overshoe. It came in two sizes and, fitted over the 16½-inch tread, it widened the tank track to 32 or to 37-inches, thereby reducing ground pressures by 30%. The grousers were made at Evansville for lack of room in any Chrysler Detroit plant.

Von Rundstedt had been thrown back and we were on the Rhine, but the war still was serious in mid-March, and General Quinton was appealing to the Corporation to exceed its March schedule of 735 tanks, with emphasis on the Pershing.

April 13th. was the fourth birthday of the original M3 pilot tank. The previous night the arsenal had built Tank No. 20,572. General Campbell wired his congratulations:

"The more than 20,000 tanks you have turned out in four years have played a key part in shifting the tide of war," the telegram read. "Today our armies are advancing along the road to victory and that advance is spear-headed by your tanks. The assembly lines of Chrysler have been basically instrumental in breaking the battle lines of the Axis. All Chrysler employees should take a personal pride in the victories of our troops, for you have played a personal part in every triumph."

No more had he sent this wire, than he was cancelling the two supplements which were to have brought tank output to 850 monthly. Though still resisting, Germany now was unmistakably whipped. Due to this and critical material shortages, the arse-

Sherman hulls, turrets and front end drive housings
stored in the open at the arsenal, November, 1943.

nal quota for 1945 was cut back from 8,881 to the still robust figure of 7,816 tanks.

Ordnance called a meeting on the 18th. of its remaining medium and heavy tank builders, Chrysler, Fisher Body and Pressed Steel Car, to fix upon the kind and numbers to be built during the rest of 1945 and in 1946. The arsenal was assigned two types of Shermans, both types of Pershings, the T92 and T93 mobile guns and the new supertank, the T29.

This latter was to weigh 57 tons net, 64 tons in battle, some 15 tons more than the Pershing. Most of this added weight would go into still thicker armor and bigger guns, either a 105-mm gun—not a howitzer—or a 155-mm howitzer. Pressed Steel Car would build a pilot model. All the arsenal ever saw of this whopper were rough layout drawings, but after VJ Day and the end of tank production, Chrysler Engineering completed the T29 design and built several of these huge tanks for the Army.

The T92 and T93 were huge self-propelled guns, the former a 240-mm howitzer on a tank chassis, the latter an 8-inch rifled cannon, about as heavy as artillery goes except in coast defense forts. The arsenal was to see these in the flesh. Chrysler Engineering designed and built four pilot models of each, the first of which reached the arsenal test track in June, 1945, before shipment to Aberdeen.

No pilot model ever had been translated from blueprints so swiftly. In a glowing letter to the Corporation on July 4, 1945, Colonel Colby wrote: "The long hours of overtime and extra manpower assigned to this task are particularly noted and appreciated. The pride of product which Chrysler, including every employee concerned, showed in finishing and perfecting this first model was exceptional and worthy of particular commendation. This office appreciated this unique cooperation. Our success in accomplishing our mission is due in no small part to such effort on your part."

Ordnance wanted that self-propelled gun in a hurry for a special purpose. The Colby letter was followed July 20th., by one from his chief, General Barnes. "I congratulate you and your organization on this

DRAWING FROM U. S. SIGNAL CORPS PHOTO

Sherman tanks for General Patton coming ashore at a French port in 1944.

General Brehon H. Somervell, Chief of Army Service Forces, and Brig. Gen. A. B. Quinton, Jr., commanding Detroit Ordnance District, with President Keller at the arsenal.

splendid 240-mm gun motor carriage," he wrote Mr. Keller. "We demonstrated this unit before officers of the 1st. Army last week, throwing direct fire against Japanese-type caves. All were most impressed with the demonstration and the functioning of this splendid unit. In fact, the test was so successful that plans are under way to send the pilot units to the Pacific as soon as all are completed. Anything you can do to speed up delivery of the rest of these pilots will be a direct contribution to the war in the Pacific."

To dispatch pilot models to the front for active service was unheard of in Ordnance, but the Jap was a burrower and we had not yet found just the right answer to his cave defenses, and only his early surrender balked these 240-mm howitzers of this distinction.

There had hung on the Works Manager's office wall since early in the war a framed poster showing a tank in action and captioned: "Help Britain Finish the Job." On the morning after VE Day, he was conferring with two lieutenants when the poster caught his eye. Snatching the May 9 sheet of his desk calendar pad, he wrote on it: "Finished," pasted this sheet on the glass of the framed poster and called for a photographer. That afternoon he sent a print of the photograph to Brigadier G. M. Ross who headed the British Army Staff office in Detroit.

The next day Ordnance slashed the arsenal's 1945 quota by 3,845 units. Before May ended, the Army wiped out what remained of the Sherman contract. Beginning June first, the working day went back to two 8-hour shifts for the first time in thirteen months. By June 15th., hourly-rate employment had fallen below 3,500 and the Corporation was moving all Government-owned tank machine tools out of Dodge, Plymouth, Jefferson and Kokomo and half of Newcastle's tank facilities.

The last 375 Sherman tanks moved out that month. Though this left the arsenal with only Pershing 105-mm models to build after August, the Army still was planning heavy tank runs in 1946 as insurance against a prolonged war in the Pacific. The Corporation had a schedule for 1946 calling for five different

69

models of which the Pershing would be the smallest.

The war ended August 14th. The next morning Chrysler had its contract termination wire from DOD —but with exceptions. The arsenal was to build 16 each of the T92 and T93, 62 more Pershings and 70 T29 supertanks. And on the second day Ordnance restored 473 cancelled Pershing tanks, plus spare parts. As of that week, the Army still intended to keep the arsenal producing under Chrysler management in 1946.

It had changed its thinking by the following week. The contract was cancelled without exceptions August 27th. The curtain was down, the rest no more than striking the scenery. Chrysler at once vacated the two top floors of the Administration building, and the Office of Chief of Ordnance, Detroit, began moving in from its scattered downtown offices.

Inventory-taking began September 5th. with materials and facilities divided into three categories

DEP'T 74 HINGES, SPROCKE BRAKE SHOES BRACKETS

A GOOD JAP IS A DEAD JAP

Tojo was hung in effigy by the arsenal workers during a bond drive.

70

*Attaching the bogie wheels to a Sher-
man tank on the arsenal assembly line.*

to be scrapped, to be shipped to other Government
arsenals or to storage, or to be held at the arsenal.

The plant which had built tanks enough to equip
more than 100 armored divisions, plus 3,126 car loads
of replacement parts, was turned back to Ordnance
October 29th. and formally accepted by Brig. Gen.
Gordon Wells, commanding the Detroit Ordnance
District postwar.

* * * * *

There was a time early in 1945 when the American
people wondered about their tanks. Though we were
winning decisively, newspaper and radio military
critics denounced the Sherman as abjectly inferior in
firepower and armor to the German Tiger and Pan-

ther tanks, quoting letters from our Armored Forces. Only our superior quantities had checked the Nazis' superior quality, they said.

And it was true that the Sherman had little chance in a slugging match with the burly German heavies. It was true that our 75-mm shells often had bounced off the thick German armor. It was true that we had no heavy tanks, nor had the British, though the Russians used them. Here was the Works Manager's own boy writing him from Germany in the Spring of 1945: "The turret of a Tiger is as big as our whole tank, and I'm not exaggerating."

But military critics should have known the answers. We were making 62-ton heavy tanks before Pearl Harbor and this M6 then, and for a considerable time after, was the world's most powerful. Our Army abandoned the type after we were at war. It did so for excellent reasons.

Our tanks had to be shipped from Detroit to the seaboard and then across an ocean and landed amphibiously on hostile shores. Here was the first limitation on size and weight. With U-boat sinkings increasing, there were not enough ships, and the bigger a tank the fewer a ship could carry. The German heavies never could have been put ashore from landing craft. Most American flat cars have a load limit of 40 tons; European flat cars are much smaller.

Our Air Force would try to destroy the enemy's bridges, and such bridges as they missed the enemy would blow up as he retreated. This meant that our armor would have to cross innumerable streams on temporary bridges. Sixty and 75-ton tanks could not have crossed such bridges.

For Germany, by then on the defensive and fighting a delaying war from interior lines, the heavy tank could be justified, though our tacticians thought that the Nazis had sacrificed most of the inherent advantages of the tank. Having many fewer tanks than us, the enemy made theirs bigger and more powerful and therefore slow and ponderous. The Tiger and the

Tank hull moving through an olive drab paint bath on the assembly line.

Installing Chrysler-built final drive and transmission. These two assemblies represented more than half the mechanical work in a tank.

Panther really were roving pill-boxes or outsize tank-destroyers rather than tanks. Two and a half hours was the maximum cruising time of some Tigers on a full load of gas.

Our armor was designed as a weapon of exploitation. We planned to and did use it in long-range thrusts deep into the enemy's rear, where it would chew up his supply installations and communications, just as Hitler's Panzers, using only light and medium tanks, had done originally in Poland, France and the Low Countries. This demanded great endurance and low gas and oil consumption at no loss in speed.

After serving for weeks in training in England, our Shermans were landed in Normandy and fought their way across France, still at full strength when they reached the Meuse in September. In exploiting a break-through, they could roll at 25 miles an hour for several hours at a time. In the Battle of the Bulge, 53 Sherman tanks of the IVth. Armored Division roared from Fenetrange in the Saar 151 miles to the Bastogne area in a day and a night.

The Germans had gone back to old-style, line-smashing, pile-up football; we were playing an open, razzle-dazzle, forward-passing tank game. Only in occasional stagnant prepared-line fighting were the Shermans unable to dodge tank-to-tank battles with the Nazi heavyweights.

Nothing but praise was heard of the Sherman until the Winter rains set in in October, 1944. By this time we had pushed the Germans back to the rough country to the south of the Rhine valley. The mud and the terrain were ideal for the Tiger and Panther. The Nazis could pick the dominating spots and post their heavy tanks there. The mud and the lay of the land prevented us from outflanking them. Our 75-mm gun was ineffective against heavy armor beyond 1,500 yards, and this was dangerously close to get to a German tank. Nevertheless, we went on winning, and with the arrival of the wide track and the long-tubed 76-mm gun with its carbide center armor-piercing shell, we recovered our original advantages over the enemy armor.

We Americans like to think of ourselves as leaders in scientific discovery. Many basic discoveries have come from Europe, however. It is in the practical application of such discoveries that we are supreme. Only we, so far, have mastered the tricks of mass production and fool-proof mechanism. Europe had a long lead with the automobile, made excellent cars for the time, but only the rich could buy them and only a mechanic could keep them running.

We began to make cars so cheaply that everyone could own one. Everyone was not a mechanic, however, nor could he afford to hire a chauffeur. And being an American, he couldn't be bothered. He demanded and got a car which would pretty well take care of itself.

The German is a master mechanic. German industry maintained its 4-year apprenticeship for every mechanic down to the last year of the war, reduced it to three years grudgingly under heavy pressure from the Army. Skilled mechanics, tool-makers and tool engineers were exempt from military service throughout. The highest quality of gauges and precision measuring devices, usually limited in this country to the tool room, were freely used everywhere in German factories.

American members of the Reparations Commission were dumbfounded after the war's end to find that

Germany had more good and new machine tools in proportion to output, population or the size and scope of its plants than we ourselves had, such a wealth of the latest tools, indeed, that they ran them only one shift a day even in the shadow of disaster. The explanation lay in a Nazi law allowing a manufacturer to write off the cost of new equipment in one year, a law deliberately intended to penalize obsolescent tools. The average depreciation write-off permitted under our tax laws is twenty years.

The Germans had the highest skills, great ingenuity, the best of tools and no lack of materials and they hid some of their most important factories under-

Adding the front drive sprockets which drive the tracks. The tank nears completion.

X-RAY STUDY OF THE INTERIOR OF
A SHERMAN TANK WITH 90 MM GUN

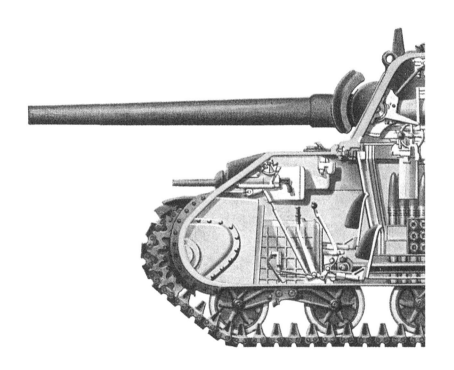

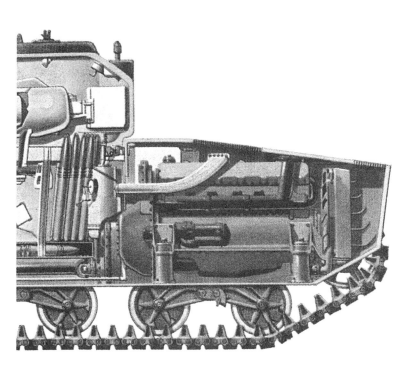

ground from our bombers. They sometimes anticipated us on fundamental improvements and they are
telling themselves that they were beaten only because we overwhelmed them with sheer masses of
men and materials.

They were not, however, whipped by quantities
alone. Our tanks were better and we used them more
intelligently. Our tanks were better because the Germans never learned to think in terms of reliability,
as we use the word, e.g.: maximum performance and
minimum care and replacement. Just as the European
pursues science for science's sake, so is he prone to
design and make machines for machinery's sake. A
captured Panzer commander grumbled that his tanks

*Tanks were rolled onto their tracks at
the end of the arsenal assembly lines.*

(*Above*) *Lowering the 30-cylinder Chrysler multibank engine into a Sherman tank.* (*Below*) *Dropping on the 5-ton turret and its gun, one of the last operations.*

Dr. Manuel Prado, President of Peru, one of many Latin-American visitors.

appeared to have been built by watchmakers. A characteristic expression in France, heard many times every day before this war, was "Ca ne marche pas", which might be translated: "It doesn't work" or "It won't run." It expressed a French if not a European philosophy. This weakness for technical prowess at the expense of dependability, simplicity and cost is shared by many American engineers, but in this practical nation the engineer is disciplined by the production man and the salesman.

No one was more outraged by the critics of the Sherman tank than was the late George Patton and no one was better qualified to reply. "In mechanical endurance and ease of maintenance our tanks are infinitely superior to any other," General Patton declared March 19, 1945.

Explaining what this meant in military effectiveness, he pointed out that the IIIrd. Army had lost 1,136 tanks between August 1, 1944, and mid-March of 1945. In the same period it had knocked out 2,287 German tanks, of which 808 were Tiger or Panther heavies. "As we always have attacked," he went on, "70% of our casualties have been from dug-in anti-tank guns, whereas most of the enemy's tanks have been put out of action by our tanks."

82

In a break-through the Tigers and Panthers were so slow that they were quickly overrun, soon out of gas and helpless. They had to be followed by corps of mechanical nursemaids and all their heavy armor being on the front slope plate and the turret, they

Sherman tanks on new test track in October, 1943. Overpass in center was part of the destroyed concrete track.

were so vulnerable on their flanks and rear that they carried into battle fourteen or fifteen infantrymen clinging to their sides. It was the duty of these foot soldiers to drop off, fan out and screen the tank from our bazooka fire. Lacking our full circle power traverse which permitted our tanks to fire in any direction, they often threw only one shell to a Sherman's three or four.

"The great mobility of the fleet-footed Sherman," General Patton continued, "usually enables it to evade the slow and unwieldly Tiger. With their adoption of this cumbersome tank, the German, in my judgment, lost much of his ability in armored combat. These tanks are so heavy and their road life so short that the German is driven to use them as guns rather than as tanks. That is, he is forced on the defensive against our armor, whereas we invariably try and generally succeed in using our armor on the offensive against his infantry, communications and supply lines, the proper use of armor.

"Had the armored division which accompanied the IIIrd. Army across France been equipped with Tigers, the road losses would have been 100% by the time we reached the Moselle river. As it was, our road losses were negligible.

"In current operations, had the IVth. Armored Division been equipped with Tiger or Panther tanks and been required to make the move from Saarguemines to Arlon, thence through Bastogne, from Bastogne to the Rhine and now to Mainz, it would have been necessary to rearmor it twice, and we should have had serious trouble in crossing the rivers."

When von Rundstedt broke through on a 40-mile

When the money was down; interior of a Sherman tank in action.

front in the Ardennes December 16, 1944, he had eight Panzer divisions. Patton, with only Sherman tanks stopped him and was attacking by December 22nd., before our overwhelming air superiority, which had been grounded by bad weather, could intervene. Anyone who still believes the German had better tanks has this crucially decisive battle to explain away. The Nazis lost so much armor and other equipment in order to gain a brief tactical success that they were fatally crippled when the Russians launched their powerful January offensive.

* * * * *

The original tank track was rubber. One set of tracks, spares included, ate up 1,734 lbs. of rubber. This forced the Army to return to steel in the Spring of 1942. A number of track patterns were then submitted to Ordnance with Chrysler liking best a rolled section originated by Mr. Weckler, and another that it called the "cuff" design.

A decision had to be reached quickly for rubber tracked shoes soon would be exhausted. It was going to be hard enough to get steel. The Works Manager

was sent to Washington to explain to General Christmas that the Corporation had these two types of track in mind. He said he believed Ordnance would adopt Mr. Weckler's suggestion eventually, but Chrysler

Assistant Secretary of State, G. Howland Shaw, hitchhikes a tank ride.

*Testing was cruel after the original con-
crete track went to pieces in May, 1943.*

could not get into production on it before the following February so it wished to tool to make the cuff
type as the only steel shoe which could be made fast
enough to replace rubber in the Fall after the first
1,000 Sherman tanks.

General Christmas approved this and within a
comparatively short time the Corporation was in
volume production of the cuff type tracks.

On December 15, the tank track committee wired
Chrysler that it wanted from the arsenal, not only
enough tracks for its 710 monthly tank quota plus
200% spares—this requirement had been doubled—

Before production all tank types were tested gruellingly at the arsenal proving grounds near Utica, Michigan.

but also 1,000 or more extra sets for other tank manufacturers.

In the interval Ordnance had adopted the Weckler rolled track and Chrysler now had verbal authorization for the facilities to make the new design, which replaced the cuff track in the Spring of 1943.

The Corporation was given a citation for the part

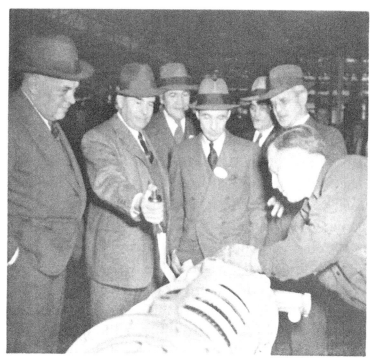

The late Edsel Ford studying a cutaway of the tank transmission at the arsenal. Matt Leonard does the explaining while B. E. Hutchinson, Chrysler Vice President and Chairman of the Finance Committee (in homburg), watches.

it played in this track emergency. "This is to certify that the Chrysler Corporation during the period from August 3, 1942, to March 31, 1943, when tank track production was very critical, made an outstanding contribution and attained unusual efficiency of production, making it possible to attain required tank schedules within the allotted time," it read.

In forwarding this citation, C. M. Burgess, as chairman of the Track Committee, wrote: "The employees of Chrysler as well as management are to be congratulated on having actually been a part of the program which contributed so largely to the success of the African and Sicilian campaigns. If the track as scheduled by Ordnance had not been produced within the allotted time, these campaigns might not have been possible."

In three months steel tracks destroyed the arsenal test track that had shown no appreciable wear in one year from the rubber soles of 4,281 tanks. The test track was a concrete figure 8 with an overpass, its purpose to give each tank a 75-mile shakedown cruise at 10 miles an hour. It took so many hours to drive 75 miles at this speed that the testing slowed deliveries. The service record of Chrysler tanks having demonstrated that this test mileage safely could be reduced, Ordnance shortly lowered the mileage and increased the permissible speeds. Still the track bore up well.

Then the first steel-shod tanks moved out of the factory October 1, 1942, onto the track. This M4 was several tons heavier than the M3 and there were many more of them, and the raised chevron bars of steel clawed and chiselled at the roadway. A cloud of cement dust hung over the track. The bridge wore through so quickly that it was closed to traffic October 16; repaved with granite blocks set in concrete. In another week, many holes began developing in the pavement on the curves and, once started, they enlarged by the hour.

Despite constant repairs, it was necessary to shut the track down New Year's Eve, an hour before the whistles blew. In 75 days' time the concrete had worn down $4\frac{1}{2}$ inches on the curves.

In the infantry any ride is better than walking—even a tank.

When the frost came out of the ground in the
Spring the patched-up cement track went to pieces
utterly and Ordnance specified a new track of 6 inches
of asphalt laid over 24 inches of gravel and macadam,
asphalt being partly self-healing and easily mended.
Between October, 1943, and the war's end, some
14,000 tanks, nearly all steel-shod, roared over the

Archbishop, since Cardinal. Francis J. Spell-man with K. T. and R. T. Keller at the arsenal.

asphalt. It was resurfaced twice, but the sub-structure never deteriorated.

From April until mid-July of 1943, however, the tanks leapt and bounced like so many chamois out of cavernous chuckholes in the old figure 8 track. The testing grew so cruel that the track was closed finally July 15th. and the tanks took their exercise around and around the big factory building on the concrete apron while awaiting the asphalt track.

Both at the arsenal and the Utica proving grounds tanks were test-driven 24 hours a day throughout the war. "Neither snow nor rain nor heat nor gloom of night stayed the swift completion of their appointed rounds." For lack of enough drivers, some had to drive ten, even twelve hours a day when engineering changes or materials shortages had backed up the arsenal assembly lines.

92

Ordnance's experimental facilities were limited to its arsenals and the 43,000-acre Aberdeen proving grounds, all overloaded, so it farmed out many hundreds of engineering projects to the Chrysler Engineering Ordnance division for a total authorization of $18,380,000.

This experimental work on tanks and other military vehicles was the principal wartime activity of the division. When the war ended, 620 projects had been completed at its big Oakland Avenue plant, 525 at its proving grounds, and a few carried over into 1946.

There is hardly a detail of the tank and its equipment that was not explored in these projects, all to the end of increasing the fighting efficiency of the weapon. The studies ranged from small laboratory investigations such as "Strength Test of Track End

Testing the Chrysler Engineering-designed horizontal volute suspension at the proving grounds before production.

U.S.S.R.'s Lt. Gen. L. G. Rudenko lunches with Vice President Hutchinson and President Keller before an arsenal tour.

Connections" at $25 to $2,291,000 for the design and building of eight pilot mobile guns. These and the pilot model of the 65-ton T32 heavy tank with its 7¾-inch frontal and 5-inch side armor, which was not completed at the Tank Laboratory until January, 1946, were the biggest, heaviest vehicles ever constructed in Detroit.

Ordnance made fifteen separate contracts with Engineering. These were unique in that no specific charge was made for the facilities; the Corporation was paid a flat $5 an hour for the services of any employee from the Zeders down. The cost of laboratory facilities, electric power, supervision and all else except materials was absorbed into this rate, to which was added a flat fixed fee of $45,000 for the duration.

Needing additional proving ground facilities, Ordnance had asked Chrysler in January, 1942, to lease the Packard automobile proving grounds near Utica, Michigan, for the testing of new types of tanks and military vehicles. The 130 Chrysler Engineering employees at Utica won their own Army-Navy E flag and a white star for a second citation. The property was returned to Packard October 27, 1945, after the exhaustive testing of 65 different types of Ordnance vehicles which logged more than 500,000 miles.

Engineering designed and built 38 different pilot tanks, many of them wholly new in type, in its Tank Laboratory. Drawings for all models after the M3, and for the innumerable changes made in these models, were released through Engineering. Dust chambers were designed and built for the Army for testing instruments. Two dynamometers capable of absorbing the whole output of a tank were built. A hot room for vapor lock and power plant cooling tests was part of the arsenal dynamometer installation. Another detail was a soundproof room into

Maj. Gen. W. W. Richards, British Army staff, garbed for a tank ride.

Assembling the long 90 mm guns into the turrets of tanks at the arsenal.

which decibel readings of all final-drive and transmission assemblies were piped and checked before assembly. Ordnance had the use of Chrysler Engineering's cold rooms, producing temperatures as low as minus 40; of its mechanical, chemical, metallurgical, structures, suspension, stress, fabrics, plastics and rubber laboratories in which the Corporation had invested many millions of dollars prior to the war.

The vertical volute suspension of the M3 tank had a short spring life, low tire mileage and insufficient flotation. The design of a better suspension was assigned to Chrysler by the Army in 1941. The result was a horizontal volute suspension used on nearly 10,000 tanks. Engineering also designed a special V-12 supercharged 1,250-horsepower tank motor which was available for Ordnance when Japan quit.

Harry Woolson of Engineering designed a new disc-type land mine exploder adopted by Ordnance. Like a disc plow, the mine exploder clears a path through mine fields, exploding the mines at no damage to itself. In the design it replaced, the discs were mounted on a common shaft and when an obstruction raised one disc it raised all. Woolson's discs were independently sprung and so overlooked no mines. In the earlier design the discs were pushed ahead of the tank and could not be steered; the Woolson exploder was steered from the tank.

Engineering designed and Utica tested the rocket

Pershing hulls starting their trip down the assembly lines in June, 1945.

launcher with which some Pershing tanks were equipped. Forty-four 4½-inch rockets were discharged in seven seconds and the cumbersome launching clusters then instantly blown off the tank and out of its path by cartridges fired from electrical controls within the tank.

One Engineering project called for the complete waterproofing of all electrical installations of the Sherman tank. A pilot tank so equipped, was returned to the Tank Laboratory in 1945 after 1,500 hours of testing in the Florida surf. Though breakers often had spilled through the open hatch, the wiring never had faltered.

Electricity and water are sworn enemies. Can you conceive of waterproofing all the complex electrical apparatus of a tank? Among the unprecedented problems were electric cable design, development of air and moisture-tight fittings for cable entrances to junction boxes, water-tight switches, junction box and cover seals, sealing of generators and motors, water-proofing of the auxiliary power plant, water-proofing instruments and panels, finding materials which would resist salt corrosion and molds.

* * * * *

Now back to the tank arsenal. The last productive work done there was the canning of a tank. Imagine a can weighing nearly 7 tons! This was part of an Army experimental program for the 50-year storage of guns and other weapons. If much of this mass of

The end of the arsenal assembly lines as the war approached its end. These are Pershing tanks. Below is a line of completed Pershings awaiting their turns on the test track.

The Duke of Windsor, former King of England, was an early visitor to the arsenal.

equipment could be stored in the open, the cost would be greatly less. Storage in the open, however, would require hermetical sealing in a protective atmosphere.

The arsenal built a huge container of steel plates welded hermetically, placing inside all the parts of a partly disassembled M4A3 105-mm tank "in such condition as to enable reconstruction of an operating tank from the store material." All parts were protectively treated. When the container had been sealed, it was exhausted through a valve and then filled with inert nitrogen gas. The pack is designed to resist temperatures from minus 60 degrees to plus 170.

The Army was exploring the possibility of storing ten million tons of equipment in this fashion. So protected, tanks and guns might be left at strategic points on our remoter frontiers, enough to hold the line or to fight a delaying action until more modern equipment could reach these outposts.

Though a tank hardly was fragile, Ordnance required during the war that it be packed as tenderly for overseas shipment as an airplane. Rust can damage, not the tank itself, but its innumerable working parts and accessories. After grease and oils, the best rust-preventive is Silica-Gel, a chemical dehydrant. The arsenal used 15,000 little bags of Silica-Gel monthly to absorb moisture in tank and tank parts packaging.

There was no mention of spare or replacement

Tanks came back from the test track to "heavy repairs" for final adjustment. These are Sherman 90 mm and 105 mm howitzer types.

*A Chrysler training school at the arsenal
graduated 3,700 Army tank technicians.*

parts in the original tank contract or the first supplement. The size of a set of spares is best suggested by the unit price, upwards of half a million dollars. In effect, parts increased a tank order by one-fourth. Making the parts was only one aspect of the problem. Chrysler set up a force of liaison engineers and sent them into the field to protect the Corporation product and aid the armored forces. These men began to report back insufficient supply and distribution of spares.

When the VIth. Armored Division moved from Camp Chaffee, Arkansas, to Louisiana and then to the California Desert Training Center to join other armored divisions on maneuvers, three Chrysler engineers went along, living with the troops. They

*The late Frank Knox, Secretary of the Navy,
with an aide and Mr. Keller at the arsenal.*

felt that Mr. Keller should see the situation for himself, and so the Corporation president arrived at
Indio in the Mojave Desert in February, 1943, slept
that night on an army cot and set out the next morning in an army car, trailing one of the armored divisions.

The Chrysler party reached the headquarters of
General Lewis, commanding the VIth., around noon.
There were no tanks there, so borrowing a Dodge
carryall from the Army, with a Chrysler liaison engi-

neer at the wheel, Keller went deeper into the desert in search of Colonel Baker, the VIth's maintenance man. From him he learned that some of the parts difficulties were intentional. The Army was deliberately simulating the conditions the armored forces might expect in North Africa.

The desert forces were divided into Red and Blue armies. Suppose that the Blues had cut off the Red army's gas supply. How would an army get gas under battle conditions if its supply line were cut? The gas would be dropped by parachutes from planes. Parachute drops do not all come down neatly in one convenient spot, however, so the Red's gasoline drums had been left here and there over the desert by trucks

Pershing 90 mm tank alongside a Sherman 76 mm. The Pershing would have been succeeded in 1946 by a 65-ton tank.

just as if they had been pushed out of planes, and it was up to the Reds to find them.

There were no more tanks at Baker's post than there had been at headquarters. The tanks were returning, the Chrysler men learned, from a 300-mile sortie and would be passing this vicinity around midnight, but Baker and his men were pulling stakes at 9 p.m. to go on ahead. This would leave the Chrysler group marooned in the desert, so they hauled out at once for the command post they had left earlier in the day. Straying off the trail, they did not stumble into headquarters until 11 p.m., to be told that the whole outfit would be moving out at 12:30 a.m. on a night march.

General Lewis and nearly everyone was asleep. The Detroiters shook out their bedrolls and lay down in the nearest empty spots, looking up at the desert stars. Before they could fall off, a soldier appeared with a pencil-like flashlight with a red lens. He shined this in the face of the sleeping soldiers who awoke and fell to.

In their carryall, the Chrysler men slipped into a line of 1,600 tanks and army vehicles, toward the head end, which moved out in blackout order. The headlights of each vehicle were pinpoints of green, the taillights two pinpoints of red. When the Chrysler driver saw the two glints of red ahead leap into the air as that car lurched through an invisible arroyo, he slowed down and felt his way cautiously through the gulley.

When he emerged on the other side, the lights had vanished. The civilians doubted that they ever should have found the column again if it had not stopped for a 5-minute rest period. From there on, the Chrysler driver set his teeth and hung grimly on the bumper of the car ahead. This went on until dawn, when the column halted for breakfast, only to resume the march at 9 a.m.

The Red and Blue armies met eventually in the concluding battle of these long and gruelling maneuvers, the clash of the tanks preceded by Red sappers clearing simulated mine fields and actual barbed wire. The Chrysler party were guests of the commanding officers in a reviewing stand run up in the

mountain pass defended by the Blues. After five days and nights in the desert, the Detroiters slept that night at Palm Springs and slept and slept.

* * * * *

Soldier students built 292 tanks under simulated field conditions in

Oliver Lucas, chairman of the Lucas (British) Commission, leaving the arsenal.

Lowering a Pershing onto a flat car for shipment. Each demanded a car with a minimum load limit of 118,000 pounds.

a Chrysler-operated Ordnance tank school housed in a small army post erected on the arsenal grounds in July, 1942. Mr. Keller had persuaded Ordnance of the value of training maintenance crews in the actual construction and assembly of tanks without the aid of power tools or cranes that they might better cannibalize tanks disabled in battle.

Twelve tanks were in course of assembly at all times, each class building two. Beginning on a Monday morning, a class would have completed both by the second Thursday. Student drivers and student inspectors drove them and checked them on Friday, the tanks returning to the shop Saturday for Government inspection and acceptance.

When the school was closed in 1944 for lack of further need, Brig. Gen. H. R. Kutz wrote Mr. Keller: "We shall always remember with deep gratitude how ably and effectively you and the entire Chrysler organization came to our aid in an hour of great need. With your whole-hearted cooperation and invaluable technical assistance, the fine facilities at your disposal were generously made available to the end that badly needed skilled Ordnance technicians could be promptly despatched to the various theaters of operation. The Ordnance training program benefitted immediately from the experience and techniques you and your staff so generously provided. The highly commendatory reports which have come back from overseas regarding the performance of the skilled technicians you trained is a sincere tribute to the

Trainload of tarpaulin-shrouded tanks moving away from the arsenal on New York Central tracks.

King Peter of Yugoslavia, since deposed, with Governor Van Wagoner and Chrysler Vice President J. E. Fields.

excellence of your product and the high standards of training maintained."

The arsenal Visitors' Book was a long and distinguished roster headed by a President and a Vice President of the United States. Easily the most spectacular of the guests were his Royal Highness, Amir Feisal, and his Saudi-Arabian entourage who stopped by on their return from the San Francisco UNO conference, but the most notable day was, of course, September 18, 1942, with the visit of President Roosevelt on a secret tour of Army camps and war plants.

*Forty-five tons of Pershing tank on the arsenal test track.
Only a few Pershings reached Europe in time to fight.*

None at the arsenal knew and very few could have guessed who was coming until the special train backed into the plant. Later in that tour, word-of-mouth reports of his coming often spread through a city despite press and radio silence, but Detroit was his first stop, the arsenal his first visit, so the secret was well kept.

It was not necessary to stage a special show for him. The test track was roaring with tanks, the plant humming normally. Except to put one tank through its paces directly in front of the Presidential automobile, there were no circus stunts and no need of them. The President, Mrs. Roosevelt and Donald Nelson rode through the arsenal aisles by car with Mr. Keller as their guide.

R. T. Keller, Chrysler Corporation Comptroller L. A. Moehring, Tank Plant Operating Manager E. J. Hunt and Chrysler Corporation Vice President and General Manager Herman L. Weckler.

Chrysler Engineering designed and built this 65-ton T-92 mobile gun for Army Ordnance.

As the secret was kept until the last day of the tour, Mr. Roosevelt made no public comment until he was back in the White House. Then he told his press conference that the arsenal "provides an amazing demonstration of what can be done by the right organization, spirit and planning."

Chrysler-built and Chrysler-motored Sherman tanks spear-headed the British recovery of Burma, moving 850 miles in 20 days through the jungle from Assam to the Irawaddy river. The British testify that the tanks and components stood up as dependably in this forbidding region as in dry and temperate climates.

113

*The late Premier Sikorsky of Poland
was an arsenal visitor in December, 1942.*

In this advance, tanks carried the infantry, foot
soldiers being unable to cut their way through the
jungle except at a crawl. When the enemy was met,
the infantry attacked as a company, leaving the tanks
unguarded against Jap suicide squads.

A letter from Burma dated May 31, 1945, said:
"In a recent action, a Jap officer climbed on the back
of a tank and struck the tank commander with his
sword, killing him instantly. He then entered the
tank and killed the gunner with his sword. The wireless operator fired his revolver but managed only to
wound the Jap. The two fell to the floor of the turret

*Chrysler Engineering also designed and built this T-93
8-inch rolling gun for the Army on a tank chassis.*

*Moisture-proof packing of spare parts. The arsenal
shipped 3,126 car loads of tank service parts.*

in hand-to-hand combat. The wireless operator managed to grab the revolver of the dead gunner and
finally killed the enemy officer."

Such instances became so common that three rifle-
men were carried on or in each tank at all times in the
later stages of this campaign.

On the bulletin board at the proving grounds there
was posted a letter from Sgt. Douglas Voigt who had
been a test driver there. It was dated at Jena, Germany, May 29, 1945.

"I had three tanks knocked out from under me," he wrote. "That is no record, but three is too many for my heart. You may think your tanks are big, heavy, thick chunks of iron, but an 88 sure makes quick work of them. They go through them just like they were a piece of paper. Twice we all managed to escape okay, but one time it got one of the boys.

"All you fellows know what a tank is like, but you never have spent 27 days and nights riding in one without relief. I did it in January and sometimes I wished we could get hit and take my chance on just getting hurt a little bit. It was during that time at Bastogne that I lost my first tank. I thought then that I would get a break, but what happened? They

General Henri Giraud between his American aide, Brig. Gen. L. J. Fortier, Chrysler Vice President and General Manager Herman L. Weckler and Brig. Gen. W. P. Boatwright, chief of the Tank-Automotive Center.

had a brand new one waiting for me when I returned to the company area. I sure cussed the production line at the arsenal for producing that one so fast."

*　*　*　*　*

H. G. Wells claims in his autobiography that he first imagined the tank in a story, "Land Ironclads," published in 1903, but steam-driven ironclads on wheels had been dreamed-up ten or fifteen years before this by writers of the American dime novel for

The late Wendell Willkie rode in a tank on a muddy day.

boys. None was made until 1916, however, and they were forced upon the British army then by Winston Churchill. Kitchener rejected them as "mechanical toys"; and when they were put into action, it was done so timidly and with so little understanding of

Grouser-equipped tank at proving grounds. These tank over-shoes were made at Chrysler's Evansville, Indiana, plant.

their possibilities that their immense value as a major tactical surprise was thrown away.

Early in World War I, Col. E. D. Swinton and others in England perceived that though the soldier could not carry bullet-proof armor, he could be carried, as the sailor was, in an armored vehicle, and that as this vehicle would have to travel across country it must move on caterpillar treads instead of wheels. So the British borrowed the American Caterpillar Tractor track, built an armored carriage which they called a "tank" in order to deceive the enemy's spies, and began September 15, 1916, at the Somme, an attempt to break the stranglehold of pill boxes and other machine gun nests in that war of fixed positions.

Tanks first were used skillfully in the Cambrai attack of November 20, 1917. Instead of the usual preliminary artillery barrage, tanks were grouped in threes as a chain of mobile armored batteries slightly in advance of the infantry. Earlier that year British casualties had risen to 8,222 per square mile gained, but from then until the end of that war casualties came down to 86 per square mile of advance.

The tank's moral effect was greater than the physical damage it did, because in the face of its assault the German soldier felt himself to be impotent, and was. Ludendorf was right when he spoke of the great tank victory at Amiens August 18, 1918, as "the black day of the German army."

But as so often in the case of great wars, it was the losing side which learned the most. Maj. Gen. J. F. C.

The Hon. C. D. Howe, Canadian Minister of Munitions, with R. T. Keller and C. B. Thomas, President of Chrysler Export.

Fuller designed a plan for the 1919 campaign, approved by Foch, suddenly to pass powerful tank forces covered by aircraft through the enemy's front to attack his supply system. As soon as the German rear should be disorganized, a strong tank-infantry frontal attack was to follow. This was the essence of the Blitz which the Nazis were to use with dismaying effect on the French nearly a generation later.

In World War I the United States had a 6-ton tank with a speed of from 3 to 6 miles an hour, closely copied from the British Mark V. Few reached France. After 1918, the Westervliet Board stressed the need of high-powered, high-speed tanks, gun mounts, personnel carriers and other military vehicles that would be independent of good roads and far more rugged and simplified in service than existing commercial vehicles. For lack of money, these recommendations came to nothing. One year Ordnance was allotted just $60,000 for tank development.

It was a private American citizen, J. Walter Christie, who developed in the early 20's the first high-speed tank. It was faster than any today, 40 to 45 miles an hour, and rode easily, but it was mechanically undependable. Perhaps if the Army had had money then it could have developed the Christie tank into what it wanted.

As late as 1931, the Aberdeen Proving Ground people were crying in the Wilderness: "Why aren't we making fast, dependable tanks and armored vehicles?" A first reason, other than lack of money, was that no engine existed which could supply the power within the weight and bulk limitations imposed. Experimental tank designs in those days were all engine, with room only for the driver and a standing gunner.

When Ordnance wished to use the new Wright radial-cooled aircraft engine, with its low weight to power ratio, the engineering profession, many aircraft engineers included, asked them how they expected to cool this motor inside a steel box. One aircraft company insisted upon designing for Ord-

This is a Sherman tank with a bulldozer earth-moving attachment

Chrysler-designed rocket launching installation being tested on tanks at the arsenal proving grounds.

nance a liquid-cooled tank motor. They produced one of reasonable weight to power ratio, but it steamed like a locomotive; it took 70 of its horsepower to cool it. When Ordnance pointed this out, the engine builders said: "Very well, we'll give you an air-cooled motor, but you'll burn it up."

Aberdeen didn't burn it up. It solved the engine problem with it, got the cooling horsepower down to 18 out of the rated 260.

By 1934 the Rock Island arsenal was producing a few M2 light tanks powered with a 7-cylinder aircraft motor and modern for their day. Wanting more

firepower and armor, Ordnance designed in 1936 the
M2 medium tank, a blown-up version of the M2
light, using a 9-cylinder aircraft engine. In 1939 Ordnance introduced a 37-mm gun and six machine guns
into the M2 medium and sent it to Fort Bragg to be
tried out by the using arms. This was the M2A1
which Chrysler set out in 1940 to make, but which
was replaced within a few days by the M3, still basically the M2 and a hurried answer to the lessons of
the Nazi Blitzkrieg.

*   *   *   *   *

The American M3 tank did not reach Africa until
the British had been driven back into Egypt, but
before the British turned on the Axis it had arrived
in numbers via the Cape of Good Hope and the Red
Sea. Let Winston Churchill testify to the decisive
part it played. Speaking to Parliament after Rommel's
Afrika Korps was in full retreat to Tunisia, the Prime
Minister said: "The Grants and the Lees stopped

*Maj. Gen. G. M. Barnes,
Ordnance Research Chief
in Washington, and Col.
William H. McCarthy,
Deputy Chief of Staff
Sixth Service Command,
with Chrysler's Director
of Research, Carl Breer.*

Part of 940 tanks returned to the arsenal for rebuilding after hard usage in training in California and Texas.

Rommel at El Alamein; the Shermans defeated him."

When Field Marshal Sir John Dill, senior British member of the combined Chiefs of Staff of the United Nations, visited the Chrysler arsenal he said: "Had it not been for the tremendous aid given by the United States, and especially the great city of Detroit, the battle of El Alamein might never have been won—or even fought."

Wavell had driven the Italians out of Cyrenaica between December, 1940, and February, 1941. Then the British halted in order to go to the aid of the Greeks. In that interval, Hitler sent Rommel with two armored divisions to the aid of his Italian ally, and the weakened British forces were swept back into Egypt, leaving a force to hold Tobruk under siege.

Churchill ordered the British VIIIth. Army to drive back to the relief of Tobruk. Lt. Gen. Sir Alan Cunningham questioned the order. Rommel had more, faster, more dependable, heavier armored and heavier gunned tanks than he. (Only 50 tanks of varying types were left in England after Dunkirk.) Having learned this at heavy cost, Cunningham recommended that the plan of campaign drawn up by his superior, General Auchinleck, Chief of the Middle Eastern Forces, be abandoned and the VIIIth. Army withdrawn for regrouping.

This led to Cunningham's removal and replacement by his deputy, Maj. Gen. Neil M. Ritchie who launched an offensive November 18, 1941, which

128

pushed the Axis back to El Agheila. But a quick counter-attack by Rommel drove the British back to the line Gazala-Bir-Hacheim.

A four months lull followed while both sides prepared to renew the battle for Egypt. Rommel logically believed that he was bound to win the race of supply and reinforcement. His supply line was short. Having lost control of the Mediterranean, British reinforcements had to move 12,000 miles around the southern tip of Africa. Troops and munitions were four to five months in transit.

Another type of tank rocket launcher. A cartridge blew it to one side after it had fired its rockets.

So when Rommel attacked May 26, 1942, Auchinleck lost 23,000 prisoners and was hurled back to El Alamein, the last and best defensive position to keep the enemy out of the Nile valley, only 60 miles away. British tank losses were disproportionately heavy. And then besieged Tobruk surrendered.

El Alamein commanded a gap of only 40 miles between the sea and the Qattara Depression, a nearly impassable salt marsh. It was a position impossible to turn and when Rommel tried on June 30th, to pierce it by frontal attack, his armor was repulsed. The next day his infantry was thrown back bloodily by the South Africans, but when the assault was renewed that night a battle-worn Indian division crumpled.

Rommel thought he had burst through and the German High Command so announced July 2, 1942, but when he tried to push on he was counter-attacked furiously and after a week he realized that he was held. At this point, Auchinleck was replaced by General Alexander, last man to leave Dunkirk and who had brought a British army safely out of Burma. Montgomery replaced Ritchie in command of the VIIIth. Army.

Alexander had been training the Xth. Army, designed as the spearhead of the reinforced British armor, far behind the lines and waiting on material.

Chrysler Engineering designed and built this improved tank mine exploder adopted by Ordnance.

When the news of Tobruk's fall reached Churchill, he was at the White House. President Roosevelt at once ordered the despatch of American M3 tanks to Egypt, withdrawing many from our own armored forces in training.

It was touch and go to get these tanks to the British in time. One of the first lots went out in a convoy of six ships. A U-boat ambush off Bermuda sank the new cargo ship Fairport with 52 tanks. Within three days the Army Transportation Corps had loaded a duplicate shipment plus much ammunition aboard the chartered Sea Train Texas.

This car ferry built for the Key West-Havana service, a 90-mile hop, skip and jump, made its way without escort around the tip of Africa and reached Alexandria while the five surviving ships of the convoy still were discharging.

Within three months of the opening of Montgomery's and Alexander's campaign in the Fall of 1942, Tripoli fell and Rommel was routed. There is no proof that they were better, bolder commanders than Cunningham, Ritchie or Auchinleck. The difference lay in Montgomery's American tanks which did to the Panzers what the Panzers had done to the British tanks—plus British recovery of control of the air, which hacked away at Rommel's supply lines.

The battle of El Alamein began in brilliant moonlight October 23, 1942, the time chosen that the in-

Tenth Armored Division tank entering the burning German town of Rosswalden.

fantry might see where it was going. It opened with an old-fashioned intensive artillery barrage such as had been discredited in World War I. In the earlier war this form of attack had been found to mean heavy casualties and a short advance against an easily reinforceable line, but Egyptian sand was not Passchendaele mud, and Rommel's line, in the short run, was not easily reinforceable, so it worked well.

Montgomery outfoxed Rommel by attacking where Rommel was strongest. Expecting the attack in his center, Rommel had concentrated his strength to one side in anticipation of hurling it against the British flank once Montgomery was well engaged.

The British infantry went first in order to clear the deadly mine fields before the tanks could move. Mines are buried just below the surface in staggered groups and are to tanks what barbed wire is to infantry. They are detected by an electrical instrument looking something like a vacuum cleaner. As each side must mark its own mine fields in order that its own forces may not stumble into them, it was customary to surround a field with a strand or two of barbed wire. This, of course, made their whereabouts as obvious to the enemy as to themselves, so many other strands were strung around pretended mine fields. The real and the false had to be felt out gingerly.

The British armor, American Grants and Lees and some Shermans, and new British Crusaders, still was practically intact while the enemy's had begun to suffer from abortive counter-attacks. The new Xth.

134

Brig. Gen. A. B. Quinton, Jr., who commanded Detroit Ordnance District, speaking at the Chrysler Tank Arsenal Army-Navy "E" award ceremony, Aug. 10, 1942.

Army, consisting of two armored divisions and a New Zealand infantry division, had been encamped in the Delta far behind the front. As far as enemy reconnaisance could tell, it still was there on October 22nd., but it had left behind a dummy camp and already was in position. The infantry had done its work by November 2nd.

When the great tank battle of El Acqaquir followed, it was won in nine hours. It ended with El

135

Acqaquir a cemetery of Axis armor. The Afrika Korps
left the Italians to take care of themselves and hardly
a man of six Italian infantry divisions escaped. The
Germans themselves lost 8,000 prisoners including a
high ranking general. The last of the enemy was out
of Egypt by November 12th.

Both the Grants and Lees were M3's, the Lee a
modification of the Grant. The Sherman was, of
course, the M4. It was the British who named them
for American generals and who first used them in
battle.

Many of these Grants, Lees and Shermans rolled
all the way across North Africa in the chase and still
were fighting in Tunisia when what was left of the
Axis armies surrendered. General Gatehouse, who

commanded the 10th. Armored division of Montgomery's Army, visited the Chrysler arsenal for the first time the following June. He told Ordnance and Chrysler men that after ten days of the El Alamein battle only his American tanks survived.

(Top) Three arsenal key men, E. J. Reis, E. C. Dodt and A. C. Breitenbeck.

Maj. Gen. R. Briggs, speaking to the School of Tank Technology in 1943, said: "After the Shermans were received it was expected that five enemy tanks would be knocked out for one British. An analysis of the El Alamein battle showed that 4.8 tanks were, in fact, knocked out for one British. Until then we should have been well content to have traded the enemy tank for tank. During the battle of Knightsbridge the M3's, which carried 100 rounds of 75-mm shells, sometimes were refilled five times within 24 hours."

(Bottom) Ecuador's President, Dr. Carlos del Rio, and son, at the arsenal.

"The Grants and the Lees have proved to be the mainstay of the fighting forces in the Middle East; their great reliability, powerful armament and sound armor have endeared them to the troops," was the statement of the Director of Armored Fighting Vehicles in the Middle East Theater before the Sherman appeared.

The Germans, whose biggest tank gun had been a 50-mm until now, already were building heavier armor, the Mark IV and the early Tiger, the Mark VI, and they rushed what they had to Africa, but there were never enough of them to influence the result. German industry could not produce them fast enough. By the time German armor was met up with again in Italy, however, it had been beefed-up in all directions and the Nazis seemed to have been convinced that the bigger a tank the better it must be.

As far back as 1940, Ordnance had wished to change the riveted hull of the M3 to a welded one, but by then all riveting equipment was on order for the arsenal and so major a change would have delayed production. This change was introduced on the Sherman. The once widely-believed story was that a shell making a direct hit on the M3 would drive the rivets inward murderously. The truth was that the advantages of the welded hull were greater strength and easier fabrication. Ordnance officers say they know of no instance of a tank crewman being wounded in this manner.

They believe this to have been German propaganda. As the changeover to the Sherman was completed, General Campbell wrote Mr. Keller: "Our M3 tanks have been so troublesome to the Germans that the enemy has concentrated the full force of his

Kwajalein Atoll, January 31, 1944. Sherman tank in support of infantry moving in on the Japs

propaganda upon them, the objective: to undermine the faith of the American people in this weapon. It has failed because the propaganda was false."

He enclosed a photograph from the London Illustrated News. The caption read: "Although they have not been long in action on the Libyan front, the U.S. General Grant tanks already have earned a brilliant reputation. Our picture taken from the inside of one of the 28-ton land ironclads as they advanced to give battle to Rommel shows, on the right hand of the driver's hatch, the barrel of the 75-mm gun which has robbed Rommel's Panzers of their hitherto superior firepower and smashed large numbers of PzIV tanks. In previous battles, the PzIV 75-mm howitzer outranged the tank guns of the VIIIth. Army, but in an early encounter eight Grants routed a force of about fifty German Mark III and PzIV tanks, fourteen of which were left on the field."

If the German military believed what German propaganda had said about the M3, which is doubtful, they changed their tune with the M4. "The German Army," an official publication, spoke almost lovingly in 1943 about the Sherman. One had been captured in Tunisia and driven 350 kilometers in $4\frac{1}{2}$ days under its own power to Tunis from where it was rushed to a proving grounds near Berlin for study.

"The armor is turtle-shaped," said the German army paper, "and is so curved and molded below the mobile turret that it appears as though human hands

140

Returned from Japanese internment, Ambassador Joseph C. Grew visits the arsenal.

had dealt in nuances rather than with the hardest type of steel . . . The mammoth rolls forward on a track the links of which are faced with rubber and, consequently, this makes for easy, noiseless and accurate operation."

The publication went on in this lyrical mood, admiring every detail of design and manufacture until, in embarrassment, it was forced to drop a crocodile tear. It was too bad, the writer said, that Americans should be so expert in production and so amateurish as soldiers. "The American effort has laid emphasis on the construction of weapons. What is lacking is manpower to utilize such material masterfully and, if need be, cold-bloodedly."

The writer did not sign his name. Did he live to see the ruins of his masterful and, "if need be," cold-blooded Reich? Did he believe what he wrote, or only wish it, suspecting even then that such a people would fight as skillfully and irresistibly for the way of life which had made such abundance possible?

If he lived, he learned that the men who fought with these weapons and the men who designed and made them, the armed and the armorers, were of the same breed.

Burning German tank.

Made in the USA
Monee, IL
17 April 2023

31989546R00085